# MEETINGS

## HOW TO HOLD 'EM
## WHEN TO FOLD 'EM

**Ruth T. Kingdon**

**Marlys E. Neis**

NOVA I, LTD., PUBLISHER
SCHAUMBURG, ILLINOIS

LIBRARY OF CONGRESS CATALOGUE CARD NUMBER:
91-090433

*First Edition: September 1991*

ISBN 0-9627557-1-0

*Illustrations by*
**Shamik Mukherjee**

# CONTENTS



WHAT DOES IT LOOK LIKE?

Successful meetings don't just happen, they're designed.



HOW DOES IT WORK?

Performance expectations that are clearly defined help to set the stage for success.



WHO SHOULD PLAY?

Meeting members themselves are the architects of effectiveness. Find the best; be the best.



WHO LEADS THE PLAY?

It all begins with the Chairperson. Organization is the key to success.

*MESSAGE   TO   THE   READER*

The way it was, is no more.   The information explosion has rocked the world with global change. Countries and cultures, beliefs and expectations are undergoing dramatic transformation.   Without information, workers were satisfied to let someone else take control.   Now, armed with knowledge, groups and individuals want to participate in making decisions. There is no turning back.   Change is inevitable . . . change is constant.

Meetings are the power tools of change.   Meetings bring our greatest resource – people – together. Meetings generate participation.   They help make decisions, find solutions and shape possibilities.  Building on the intellect and creativity of people is the potential that meetings offer.   Whether that potential is achieved depends on *how* we meet.

We are hovering on the brink of the future.   Would you bet your future on the quality of *your* meetings?

v

*To powerful meetings . . .*

**MEETING:** an assembly; a gathering of people, especially to discuss or decide on matters. (Webster's)

**CHAPTER 1**

# THE WINNING HAND

Regardless of where we live or what we do, our lives are orchestrated by meetings. We meet to plan, coordinate, evaluate, resolve, inform, instruct, create . . . Every organization, whether social, professional, governmental or business uses meetings as one means of handling and managing its affairs. It's little wonder that as we are bombarded with rapid change and chaotic schedules, the last thing we want to face is one more meeting.

Yet meetings *can* produce dramatic results. The stimulation of a group often revives sagging motivation and defeats humdrum attitudes. Because interaction sparks ideas, the fastest way to a sure solution is frequently found in the imagination and intelligence of a group.

If meetings are so important, why do so many feel like such a waste of time?  Too often our meetings are treated like "events" that require an hour or two of our time.  Rarely do we remember that meetings demand an investment before, during and after the actual event.  A successful meeting does not begin with the call to order and end with adjournment.  Agreeing to meet is but one portion of the total commitment.  To be effective, meetings require dedication to the process as well as the event.

The responsibility for impressive results rests with all members of the group; each person contributes to the success or failure of the whole.  Accepting this responsibility requires an investment of time and attention.  Yet every investment is a risk; there are no guarantees that any meeting will yield a "fair return."  The stakes are high!


## THE CHIPS:  WHAT CAN YOU LOSE?

TIME.  Let's face it, meetings can pose an incredible threat to our productivity and our ability to get the job done.  Many of the meetings that we attend *are* a waste of time.  Since time is one of our most valued and endangered resources, it pays to make sure that your time will be well spent *before* agreeing to invest it!

MOTIVATION.  Bad meetings can destroy incentive, sabotage forward motion and discourage and deflate participants.  Disorganization and disinterest can demolish commitment. Meetings can wipe out as well as build motivational resources and energy.

MONEY. Bad meetings are more than a drag . . . they're a drain!  The outright dollar investment of the average meeting is rarely considered.  Yet, careful addition of only the hourly wage of those in attendance, would stagger the average attendee.  The potential outcome is not always worth the dollar investment.

## THE POT:  WHAT DO YOU STAND TO GAIN?

UNDERSTANDING.  Direct involvement replaces "they" with "we."  The first-hand experience provided in a meeting creates a common understanding and appreciation of the problems  and the issues that's hard to find elsewhere.

COMMITMENT.  Meetings personalize decisions. Participation gets people involved and stimulates ownership.  Ownership breeds a commitment that's personal and real.

PERSPECTIVE.  Meetings bring all sides of the issue into focus.  This helps to minimize misunderstandings, clarify reality and balance biases.

SUCCESS.  The combined experience, knowledge and perspective of the group produces impressive results. Success means more ideas generated, more problems solved, more projects conceived and achieved.

# THE ACES

Meetings represent a big investment.  The stakes *are* high.  Time, energy, and money are the chips we use; resources wasted are opportunities lost.  Because of the risks, each investment deserves careful consideration. Whether we win the pot or lose our chips, the choice is ours.

Good meetings require teamwork.  Shared responsibility develops commitment and helps to prevent the frustration caused by non-productive meetings or meetings that really didn't need to happen. Before getting involved, make sure that the stakes are on your side.  Look for the ACES:

1.  DIRECTION.  A clear reason for meeting; leadership that shows.

2.  PREPARATION.  Plans to make the best use of the time; performance that delivers.

3.  PARTICIPATION.  Exchange that produces ideas; dialogue that promotes understanding.

4.  ACTION. Commitment to achieve success; the power and expertise to make it happen.

## DIRECTION

Is this meeting really necessary?  How many times have you heard yourself saying those words, or worse yet, thinking those thoughts as you sat mesmerized, bored, frustrated or infuriated in yet another meeting?  Good direction ends the "why am I here" dilemma before it begins.

The direction of successful groups is evident before, during and after the meeting.  Direction requires:

- COMMUNICATION.  Good direction is supported by impeccable communication that tells participants what to expect and what's expected of them.

- LEADERSHIP.  Direction is heavily influenced by one person:  the appointed chairperson.  Confident leadership is able to aim the group and keep it on target and on time.

- PURPOSE.  Direction begins with clear goals.  Goals that are simply and directly stated instruct members regarding the desired end-point, as well as what will be required to achieve "success."

## PREPARATION

"I forgot."  "I didn't have time."  "I didn't know."  "I didn't understand . . ."  How many excuses for being ill-prepared have you heard?  How many have you used?

Preparation improves the quality of discussion and decisions and reduces the time required to meet. Preparation doesn't just happen; it's planned, encouraged and stimulated. Preparation begins with:

- COMMUNICATION. Objective, clear, consistent and reliable communication gets results.

- CONSIDERATION. Consideration – of the chairperson by the rest of the group – and of the rest of the group by the chairperson supports preparation. Helping others meet responsibilities, helps everyone. "Lead time" is always respected within the considerate group.

- ENCOURAGEMENT. Preparation is fed by encouragement. Difficult projects and complicated issues consume lots of energy. A pat on the back, an understanding ear or a little stroke help to restore enthusiasm.

- PLANNING. Careful planning assures that the right issues are discussed at the right time and that the information needed to assure action is available at the meeting.

- ORGANIZATION. Effective meeting orchestration requires careful organization. Organization shows in the anticipation that is given to meeting discussion and the way that all details are managed. Organization makes resources needed, including time, part of the planning process.

## PARTICIPATION

The exchange stimulated by the group interaction is what distinguishes meetings from other forms of communication. Yet in many meetings expression is not only discouraged, it's prevented. Two-way, all way communication is the essential ingredient in participation. The positive exchange of ideas is promoted by:

- ATTENDANCE. Effective participation begins with interaction. For interaction to occur, members must show up for meetings.

- ATTENTION. Attention is critical to productive participation; it's the concentration that helps move business to conclusion quickly and efficiently. Attention conserves time and reduces frustration.

- BALANCE. The ability to say what one feels is central to effective participation. When power and opinion are balanced, all members feel secure in expressing their opinions. Willingness to examine all sides of the issue is supported and promoted .

- FAIRNESS. Fairness empowers the whole and lets participation occur; it makes everything "equal" inside the meeting room.

## Action

Commitment to do more than merely talk is critical to the success of a meeting. Talk is just talk until action occurs. Doing "something" strengthens the sense of accomplishment for participants. Even if "something" is simply communicating the results, the cycle must be completed. Action is never guaranteed. However, action is influenced by:

- Clarity. Groups that achieve results have a precise vision of their goal(s). Ambiguity is a roadblock to action. Action needed must be directly stated and consistently communicated if it is to be achieved.

- Commitment. Issues that are important to the individuals involved stimulate commitment to act. Commitment creates the *want to* necessary to overcome the inertia of procrastination.

- Expertise. Logically, "know how" leads to better results. Expertise needed for action includes first hand knowledge/experience with the issues central to the meeting as well as technical skill.

- Power. Power to act improves the probability of success. Groups that have either been granted the authority to act or that hold the potential to influence others are more likely to succeed. Without power, decisions dead end inside the meeting room door.

## *Your Responsibility . . .*

Meetings represent a big investment; making this investment pay off is both our opportunity and our responsibility.  The Pot we can win promises solutions backed by understanding, ownership and commitment.  The Chips we can lose waste our most valuable resources – time and energy.  Meetings are an expensive and risky investment.

Successful meetings don't just happen – they're *designed:*  The chapters that follow provide tips and tools that can help to keep the ACES in your hand and stack the deck in your favor *every* time you pull up to the table.

*Go For Broke!*

**Play by the Rules!**

## CHAPTER 2

# THE RULES OF THE GAME

Are your meetings tightly organized or do they wander because expectations haven't been defined? Too many unbreakable rules can lead to rigidity and ineffectiveness. Too few rules can produce disorganization and delay. "The Aces" – DIRECTION, PREPARATION, PARTICIPATION AND ACTION – are reinforced when performance expectations are clearly defined.

"Rules of the Game" provide new members an understanding of responsibilities and give potential members a glimpse of the commitment that's needed.

Expectations strengthen contributions and serve as a guide for member development.  "Rules of the Game" may vary according to the purpose of the group or the style of the leader.  The manner in which expectations are structured, however, sets the tone for the group.

The rules presented in this chapter represent minimum expectations.  Sections are meant to stand alone as the basis for instruction regarding role responsibilities or to be used collectively as the framework for achieving the maximum benefit from any meeting that is held.

The "Winning Hand" requires winning hands:  each person has a part to play if DIRECTION, PREPARATION, PARTICIPATION AND ACTION are to be achieved.  Well-defined and clearly stated expectations prompt the actions that are critical to success.

## LEADING THE PLAY

The Chairperson leads the game and helps to keep things moving.  It's the Leader who can ignite the room with energy or fill the room with disinterest.

Although the Chairperson is not solely responsible for the meeting and its outcomes, the leader does exert the greatest amount of control over the events that occur inside the meeting room.  Defining leadership responsibilities makes it easier for all who assume the role to understand what's expected and to know what to do.

## CALL THE GAME

Meetings begin and end with direction.  Direction is expressed in virtually everything that the leader does.  It's the leader, the appointed Chairperson, who clarifies the purpose and direction of the group most consistently.

The challenge of the chair becomes easier when the mission of the group is clear to all who are present.  One of the leader's primary responsibilities, then, is to supply direction.  The manner in which direction is achieved and maintained sets the tone for group productivity.  The best leaders show the way through artful application of the "Rules of the Game."

- FOCUS THE GROUP.  Make sure everyone knows the purpose of the meeting.  Communicate the mission all ways, always.

- PRIORITIZE THE ISSUES.  Make sure that the right issues are handled at the right time.  Important issues first.

- EXPLAIN THE RULES.  Define expectations, rules of order and the decision-making process.  Determine the right amount of "Law and Order" within the room.  Make sure that everyone understands how the meeting process will be managed.

- Activate Exchange.  Define channels for making suggestions, giving input and reviewing progress. Make sure everyone understands how to communicate between meetings as well as during meetings.

- Express Enthusiasm.  The leader is the mirror. Groups reflect the attitudes and approaches of their leaders.  Make sure that messages given are the ones that are intended.  Consider the needs of the group before your own.  Enthusiasm helps to move the group toward the goal without pushing, pulling or shoving.

- Show the Way.  Show members what you expect. Set the example.  Be prepared for the meeting, be enthusiastic, transmit optimism.  Arrive early to meet, greet and set the tone.

**Be ready for the deal**

Leaders set the stage for using the meeting *process* instead of only the event.  The leader makes it clear that preparation contributes to meeting effectiveness; the leader organizes to assure that preparation can occur and coaches to help it happen.

Good preparation requires more than merely completion of tasks; it requires consideration of the issues and anticipation of the discussion as well.  This kind of preparation is not realized by simply demanding – it comes from inspiration and example.  Leaders don't just expect preparation, they inspire it.

- ANTICIPATE DISCUSSION.   Identify and outline information that may facilitate discussion and speed resolution.   Assign group members to research and bring the data needed.

- PLAN AHEAD.  Give thought to how much time will be required to review the issues and prepare for discussion.  Distribute agendas in advance; allow participants the chance to project and prepare for discussion.

- SHARE EXPECTATIONS.  Make it clear.  Make sure that everyone understands what's needed.  Specify the preparation that's required on the agenda, via memo, call or conversation.

- GUARANTEE RESULTS.   Follow-up, check on key progress points.  Help individuals who seem to be "stuck" or who need a hand.  Make sure it all comes together at the appointed time.

## DEAL EVERYBODY IN

The leader creates the atmosphere that invites interaction.  It's the leader who can instill the group with the desire to take part, to join in.  Creating the desire to participate involves more than merely orchestrating the discussion; it includes nurturing the process before, during and after the event.  Good participation begins with fairness and a commitment to include everyone.

Groups quickly sense the leader's attitudes. The wrong tone can contribute to a "Why bother?" mentality that destroys effective participation. For leaders who earn the respect of their groups, participation becomes a team effort characterized by a strong esprit de corps. For leaders who don't play by the rules, participation can become a source of frustration and aggravation.

- BE FAIR. Make sure that all opinions are heard and that discussion is not biased before it begins.

- INSPIRE CONTRIBUTIONS. Give all members a chance to contribute:  draw out the quiet, calm the boisterous, balance the bold. For meetings that include multiple sessions, use the time between meetings to talk with individuals who need to be drawn out – or who require "toning" down.

- PURSUE PROGRESS. Point out the goal. Rescue discussions from tangents. Keep hidden agendas or personal interests from interfering with the primary purpose of the group.

- CAPTURE ATTENTION. Make sure the room is inviting, appropriately arranged and adequately comfortable for the business that needs to occur. Promote participation with eye contact; arrange the chairs for face-to-face discussion. Consider group needs when scheduling the meeting time and place; pick a productive and convenient time and a spot with minimal distractions.

## WIN THE GAME!

"Achieving begins with believing." Leaders know what must occur for results to be realized and help the group to create a vision of success. Leaders avoid using mistakes as opportunities to chastise or embarrass individuals. Leaders believe in their groups: they not only believe that action is possible, but that it is certain.

The leader uses the power and expertise of the group to get results. The leader helps the group achieve success by nurturing and coaching, not by driving, belittling and badgering. The leader demonstrates confidence that the mission of the group can be accomplished, and that the participants are capable of attaining the goal.

- FOCUS ON RESULTS. Make progress the goal and mistakes learning opportunities. Don't dwell on what didn't work or who was wrong; focus instead on what might work and what to try next.

- CULTIVATE EXCELLENCE. Teach members how to meet expectations and complete actions needed. Coach to success.

- NUDGE TOWARD THE GOAL. Make sure that everyone "remembers" responsibilities. Remind and encourage when necessary.

- LEAD THE WAY. Never ask anyone to do something that you wouldn't do yourself. Be prepared for meetings, model enthusiasm for the project. Inspire commitment: communicate belief in the purpose and in the group. Help the group to believe.

## CONTRIBUTING TO THE POT

Whether chosen because of job title or by virtue of expertise, all members have a specific function to fulfill. Everyone is required to participate: meeting is an active, not passive word.

Accountability begins with understanding the obligations; basic responsibilities must be shared and explained. Informed and involved members shape the best meetings.

### KNOW WHY YOU'RE AT THE TABLE

It's basic. To make effective contributions, one must know the purpose of the meeting. This knowledge must translate to understanding and commitment. Results are dependent on the "drive to the goal" demonstrated by the group.

Although the Chairperson is responsible for communicating the purpose, understanding is individual. "I didn't know" – or – "They didn't tell me" – are not excuses for failing to comprehend. If you don't understand, ask. It's your time; it's your responsibility.

Personal agendas and ulterior motives can destroy commitment to the common purpose and waste group time. Those who take part must play by the rules of the group. Members who play by the "Rules" agree to respect the role and responsibilities of the Chairperson.

- IDENTIFY THE TARGET. What is this group supposed to achieve? Turn the purpose into a mission for everyone.

- STICK TO THE TOPIC. Redirect tangential discussions when they occur. Make sure your own contributions are germane to the discussion.

- KNOW YOUR ROLE. What is it that you have to offer to the group? Why are you at the meeting?

- PLAY BY THE RULES. Talk with - not about - people; deal with issues, not personalities. Support established group rules.

## BE READY FOR THE DEAL

Preparation is part of the commitment. Taking part in a group project means agreeing to allocate time for preparation as well as attendance. Preparation requires planning. For some this necessitates actually scheduling time on the calendar; for others getting the agenda and the background materials to the bedtime reading pile is sufficient.

Preparation requires self-discipline. Procrastination is the most common form of meeting sabotage. Good intentions and "I meant to's" don't help move projects; action does. Issues that are important get time. Make each commitment important enough to eliminate the excuses and deliver the results.

One of the final steps in preparation is the gathering of materials. Think ahead. Organize. Nothing is more frustrating than to waste time because "I don't have what I need." Anticipate and prepare for participation.

- RESERVE THE TIME. Budget time for attendance *and* preparation when the meeting is scheduled.

- STUDY THE PLAY. What do you do best? Where is your contribution most needed?

- SHARE YOUR STRENGTHS. Let others know what you do well; offer to help.

- COMPLETE YOUR ASSIGNMENTS. What's expected of you? By when? How much is independent work and how much requires work with others? Schedule the time for *complete* preparation.

- ANTICIPATE DISCUSSION. Review the agenda, research the issues. Organize for contribution to the group. Share information that you have with others; don't wait to "dump" it at the meeting.

- OFFER A HAND. When others are struggling, offer to help them out. Let them know what you can do to help with their preparation.

## Ante Up!

Participation requires active exchange of information and ideas; it means interaction, not taking over or just "being there." Involvement requires action; it doesn't just "happen."

Attendance is basic to interaction. The absence or the habitual tardiness of one individual can delay or even stop the progress of the group. Appearing on time, every time, demonstrates respect for others and a commitment to the cause.

Those interested in getting the most out of their time promote a sense of fair play. Biases and personal agendas do not belong in the meeting room. The best members promote objectivity that leads to results that work.

Keeping the discussion on track speeds goal attainment. Each member shares the onus for redirecting runaway discussions; each is responsible for maintaining his own commitment to the goal.

- Be There! Attendance is an ingredient necessary for participation that is all too often minimized or ignored. Absence or sporadic attendance leaves a void in the group that inhibits consistent forward progress. Make the commitment to "do the time" – or don't make the commitment.

- Contribute to the Discussion. Make sure your viewpoint is adequately understood.

- PLAY FAIR.   Don't get swept away with the moment; point out biases when they occur. Encourage examination of the other side.

- DEAL WITH FACTS. Discourage generalizations, encourage rational review of the facts.

- PROMOTE UNDERSTANDING.   Asking the right question is often as valuable as having the right answer.

- LISTEN.  Absorb the viewpoints of others; devote at least as much effort to understanding their viewpoint as to expression of your own.


## PUT YOUR CARDS ON THE TABLE!

Whether expert or novice, the contributions to the group become most evident when results are produced. Results demand action.   Action translates into completion of assignments, follow through on decisions, and communication of conclusions.

Meeting results are enhanced when teamwork is present.  An air of "if you succeed, I succeed" must be present.  Team players help others to succeed.

- COMMIT TO THE GROUP.  Voice disagreements inside the meeting, but commit to follow through on group decisions after the meeting.

- MOTIVATE, INSPIRE OTHERS.  Help others to believe in the cause and the group enough to get involved and "make something happen."

- PRODUCE RESULTS.  Follow through on your commitments.  Don't promise if you won't or can't invest the time to complete the work.  Don't be responsible for the detour that delays the group.  If you can't deliver like you said you would, tell someone;  communicate  directly  to  the Chairperson as soon as possible.

## KEEPING SCORE

Yes, meetings mean minutes as well.  Minutes serve as a "Score Card" to communicate results and answer questions later.  They help to promote team understanding by providing a vehicle for communication and coordination.  Good minutes support forward progress.  Post meeting responsibilities are clearly documented and serve as a reminder to all.  Because of these functions, minutes should present an accurate, objective picture of the meeting and its outcomes, and they should be available as soon after the meeting as possible.

A scorecard is an essential part of the game . . . but should not be allowed to become an overwhelming chore or needless documentation of detail.  Listening for the key points can be everyone's responsibility.  A skillful chairperson will assist by clearly summarizing each issue following discussion.  When it comes to actually taking minutes, try a flip chart, a tape recorder, a form – or even a laptop computer! The point is, document what's needed in the most efficient manner possible.

What's needed? The basic rules for scorekeeping are simple and direct: minutes should be simple and direct as well. Employ a format that's easily understood. Use lists, highlight decisions; make later review for key points a snap. Good minutes:

- NAME THE GAME. Why was the meeting held? Whether the meeting was a routine business meeting or an ad hoc group assembled to address a specific problem, make sure the minutes include a succinct statement of purpose.

- IDENTIFY THE PLAYERS. Who came? Include first initials and last names so that later identification is not confusing.

- DESCRIBE THE PLAY. What issues were raised? What discussion occurred? Include issues in list form or use concise sentences that summarize the key points. Focus on the concepts and issues, don't get bogged down in details that aren't critical.

- ADD UP THE SCORE. What decisions were made? What actions are needed? Who will do what? By when? Describe the action that was taken and the action that will be needed in specific terms.

- CALL THE NEXT DEAL. Will there be another meeting? When will it be held? Where will it be held? Make sure that further actions are defined.

## *Play by the Rules?*

Responsibilities that are unmistakably clear improve meetings.  The best meetings are those in which each person accepts responsibility for making the "The Winning Hand" a reality. When expectations are understood and executed, the probability of success is increased.

It all begins and ends with the Chairperson.  The leader is responsible for focusing the group, prioritizing the issues, explaining the rules and activating the exchange.  It's the leader who sets the stage for using the meeting process.    The Chairperson anticipates discussion and shares expectations for preparation, participation and action with the group.

From maintaining focus to taking positive action, members share the responsibility for making the meeting a success. Procrastination and personal agendas are not allowed in the daily game of meetings. Everybody plays, and everybody plays fair.  When the players know the rules, the value of the investment is increased.

Will your meetings be organized or will they wander because no expectations have been defined?  Increase your odds:

*Play by the Rules!*

# IN SUMMARY

---

TO LEAD THE PLAY:

1. *Provide direction:  Name the Game*
   - Focus the group
   - Prioritize the issues
   - Explain the rules
   - Activate exchange
   - Express enthusiasm
   - Show the way

2. *Assure Preparation:  Be Ready for the Deal*
   - Anticipate discussion
   - Plan ahead
   - Share expectations
   - Guarantee results

3. *Inspire Participation:  Deal Everybody in*
   - Be Fair
   - Inspire contributions
   - Pursue progress
   - Capture attention

4. *Guarantee Action:  Win the Game*
   - Focus on results
   - Cultivate excellence
   - Nudge toward the goal
   - Lead the way

SUMMARY CONT'D.

To CONTRIBUTE TO THE POT:

1. *Uphold direction: Know why you're at the table*
   - Understand the objectives
   - Stick to the topic
   - Know your role
   - Play by the rules

2. *Prepare: Be ready for the deal*
   - Reserve the time
   - Study the play
   - Share your strengths
   - Complete your assignments
   - Anticipate discussion
   - Offer a hand

3. *Participate: Ante up!*
   - Be there
   - Contribute to the discussion
   - Play fair
   - Deal with facts
   - Promote understanding
   - Listen

4. *Act: Put your cards on the table*
   - Commit to the group
   - Motivate, inspire others
   - Communicate your progress
   - Produce results

## SUMMARY CONT'D.

### TO KEEP SCORE:

1.  Name the game
2.  Identify the players
3.  Describe the play
4.  Add up the score
5.  Call the next deal

The length of a meeting rises with the square of the
number of people present.

## CHAPTER 3

# THE PLAYERS

How are your committees appointed? "It's *your* turn" – "It's your job?" – "You've been volunteered. " – Or do you have people standing in line to make a contribution?

When meetings are viewed with dread or indifference, it's difficult to find anyone who is willing to accept the responsibility and devote the time. Attendance is assumed by default; securing sensational participants is left to chance.

## TURNING THE TABLES . . .

Because people are the active ingredient in meetings, it's important to get the right combination. Recruiting the best is hard if meetings are viewed as burdens.  To move from drudgery to opportunity requires a change in the way that we look at the process. Meetings must be seen as a valuable use of time; "chore" must be replaced with "aspiration." When there's confidence in the outcomes that can be achieved, finding the best is easy . . . because the best are always available.

Turning the tables demands attention in three areas:

1.  TEACH THE GAME.  Does everyone understand the purpose of meetings?  Do they know how to get involved and how to be a productive member? Make sure that everyone comprehends the "Rules of the Game."

2.  BROADCAST THE POT.  What results are achieved because of meetings that are held?  Attract participation because of what gets done.

3.  INVITE THE CRITICS.  Are changes made to correct the "bad" and learn from the "good" – or do things just go on like they always have, regardless of the need for improvement?  Make evaluation an important part of the meeting; let the participants help to mold the process.

## TEACH THE GAME

For those who hate to go or never attend, it helps to know what to expect as well as what's expected.  A simple orientation for new members and for new groups can solve a lot of later problems.  Furthermore, when education about meetings and their importance is available to everyone, the stage is set for tapping and using the collective intelligence of all.  Meeting education should:

- ACTIVATE COMMITMENT.  Explain the importance of meeting and produce the desire to get involved.

- STIMULATE INTEREST.  Arouse interest based on the opportunities that are available.  Make participation come to life with specific descriptions of needs.

- SPARK ENTHUSIASM.  Create energy for the process by sharing examples of results that have been achieved.

- INSPIRE IMPROVEMENT.  Specify how each individual can improve the effectiveness of meetings that are held.  Teach the "Rules of the Game."

- PRODUCE RESULTS.  Explain how and when to get involved.  Make action needed clear.  Produce interested volunteers.

## Broadcast the Pot

What's in it for me? Does it really make a difference? Getting the best representatives is directly dependent on the enthusiasm generated by the success of previous meetings. When everyone begins to see that involvement and influence *do* make a difference, the enthusiasm and interest in meetings increases. Put another way, nothing feeds success like success! Making a difference, having influence, is important. The challenge then, is to make sure that involvement demonstrates "a difference" and that everyone understands what that difference is. To capitalize on the infectious process:

- Publicize Results. What changes have been made as a result of meetings that have been held? How effective are the groups that meet? Tell everyone.

- Recognize and Reward Involvement. Give credit, make sure that those who do get involved are recognized for their efforts and their accomplishments.

- Make Getting Involved Fun. Promote a sense of enjoyment inside meeting rooms. Make meetings opportunities for feeding creativity with fun. Encourage the use of humor with a relaxed atmosphere that's directed at achievement.

## Invite the Critics

When things didn't or aren't working as planned, everyone in the meeting loses. Having the opportunity to improve and correct meetings that aren't working empowers those in attendance. This strength boosts interest in future meetings by showing that involvement *can* make a difference. To encourage meeting evaluation and improvement:

- Create Opportunity. Give everyone (members and others) a chance to offer suggestions for improvement. Develop evaluation methods, promote evaluation opportunities. Make sure everyone understands how to express opinions and make recommendations.

- Show Flexibility. The freedom to be spontaneous, to try "something else if this fails" is essential. Systems that are flexible stimulate feedback. Everyone should understand that sacred cows and immovable objects are obsolete. Suggestions should be encouraged, welcomed and seriously considered.

- Promote Progress. Publicize the successes and failures in meetings. Show how suggestions are used to make each and every meeting the best possible.

# STACKING THE DECK

The best meetings result from the right combination of chemistry, experience and knowledge. Selecting individuals who will represent the most complete perspective most effectively and efficiently can be a challenge. When faced with difficult choices, it's best to look for those individuals who can help to achieve DIRECTION, PREPARATION, PARTICIPATION AND ACTION.

1.  **DIRECTION** – Participants who will focus on the real problems and issues; who help others to reach for the goal:

    *   REFLECT CONCENTRATION. They're able to zero in on the issues without being distracted by outside concerns and pressures.

    *   COMMIT TO THE PURPOSE. They're willing to forego personal agendas to achieve the goals of the group.

2.  **PREPARATION** – Individuals who will devote energies to preparation and help others to do so as well:

    *   DEMONSTRATE ORGANIZATION. They are able to allocate and budget time; see the whole as well as the detail of the tasks to be done and can, thus, organize the *total* work to be done.

- SHOW CONSIDERATION.  They understand the pressures of others and are willing to lend a hand, bend, to achieve the desired results.

3.  PARTICIPATION – Those who will promote effective interaction:

  - DEMONSTRATE OBJECTIVITY.  They are skilled at presenting unbiased perspectives of the issues.

  - ENJOY EXCHANGING IDEAS.  They communicate thoughts clearly and eagerly.

  - DISPLAY SELF-CONFIDENCE.  They're sure of themselves and are comfortable expressing ideas and opinions to others.

  - COMMIT TO ATTEND.  They know that participation cannot occur if they don't attend; they agree to invest the time.

  - EXHIBIT RECEPTIVITY.  Ideal participants are open to new ideas and remain open-minded in spite of personal interests and beliefs.

  - PROMOTE COOPERATION.  They like to work with others and display friendly cooperative attitudes when placed in a group setting.

**4.** ACTION – Individuals who will actually commit to action:

- DISPLAY INTEREST. They *care* about the outcome and are genuinely concerned about the topic at hand.

- DESIRE CLOSURE. They work hard to demonstrate results and have a "track record" of achieving results and closure with other projects.

- DISPLAY OPTIMISM. They're willing to look for solutions when all that others see are walls; they help others move past self-limiting beliefs and dead-end tangents to positive solutions and impressive accomplishments.

- DEMONSTRATE EXPERTISE. They possess knowledge, technical ability or political savvy necessary to achieve the necessary outcome.

- EXPRESS DETERMINATION. They have a clear commitment to investing the time necessary to get the job done.

## BECOMING THE PERFECT PLAYER

Let's face it.  Few, if any of us, qualify as the "perfect member" every time we pull up to the table. Getting involved is not always easy.  Whether for want of opportunity to present issues in a group setting, or lack of genuine interest in the issue(s), participation often falls flat.  The fact is, good participation is developed.  It doesn't just "happen."  The key to success is to work always at *becoming* rather than being content to merely "be."  To improve your "perfect member" quotient:

- KNOW YOURSELF.  What are your strengths?  What are your weaknesses?  Think about the meetings you've attended; think about the groups with which you're currently involved.  What's your role within the group?  Whatever your basic personality or interaction tendencies, no improvements can be made until you understand what effect you have on others and how you can improve that effect.  Make notes about how you feel you perform in a group. Try to imagine how you are viewed.  Verify your impressions: talk to others.  Ask about their reactions to you and your performance.

- OBSERVE OTHERS.  Identify others who have strengths and abilities that you would like to emulate. Study them. Talk with them. Adopt a mentor.

- CLARIFY EXPECTATIONS. Know what's expected. If you don't understand, ask. If you know and someone else seems to be floundering, help them. Make sure that what "everybody knows" is really *understood* by everyone.

- COMMIT TO EXCELLENCE. Going through the motions does not produce excellence. Believing in what you're doing and the reason that you're doing it produces excellence. Make sure that you can make the commitment in spirit as well as time and energy before agreeing to meet.

- PLAY TO YOUR STRENGTHS. Wise individuals know which issues will be within the range of their abilities and time. Make sure that the commitments you make are commitments that you can fulfill. If this project feels like it's not in your range, suggest someone who may be able to meet the responsibility more effectively.

- COMMIT TO COMPLETION. "It's not over until the fat lady sings." Make sure that the results that are to be achieved are actually achieved. Don't give up before the last ounce of effort has pushed the project over the top.

## *Make it Work!*

Good meetings require good participants.  Whether your group is just being appointed or solidly entrenched, the perfect player can be found or created.  The key is to cultivate enthusiasm:  make sure that everyone knows why involvement is important and how they can get involved.  Clarify the "Rules of the Game."  Evaluate: give everyone an opportunity to help shape the direction of future meetings.

Good meetings are supported when members make a personal commitment to growth.  Individuals must be willing to find out what has to change to make things better; they must understand how they contribute or detract from the whole.

It takes courage to accept the challenge to become rather than merely be.  It requires a commitment to yourself and others.  Good meetings don't just happen, they're designed – and the members themselves are the architects of effectiveness.  Don't let the status quo form an anchor around your neck: be the one that makes a difference!

*Make it Work!*

# IN SUMMARY

TO INCREASE INTEREST IN MEETINGS:

1. *Teach the Game*
   - Activate commitment
   - Stimulate interest
   - Spark enthusiasm
   - Inspire improvement
   - Produce results

2. *Broadcast the Pot*
   - Publicize results
   - Recognize and reward involvement
   - Make getting involved fun

3. *Invite the Critics*
   - Create opportunity
   - Demonstrate flexibility
   - Promote progress

TO FIND THE BEST MEMBERS LOOK FOR:

1. *Direction – Those who:*
   - Reflect concentration
   - Commit to the purpose

2. *Preparation – Those who:*
   - Demonstrate organization
   - Show consideration

SUMMARY CONT'D.

3.  *Participation – Those who:*
    - Demonstrate objectivity
    - Enjoy exchanging ideas
    - Display self-confidence
    - Commit to attend
    - Exhibit receptivity
    - Promote cooperation
    - Display interest

4.  *Action – Those who:*
    - Desire closure
    - Display optimism
    - Demonstrate expertise
    - Express determination

TO BECOME THE BEST THAT YOU CAN BE:
- Know yourself
- Observe others
- Clarify expectations
- Commit to excellence
- Play to your strengths
- Commit to completion

**YOU'RE IT!**

## CHAPTER 4

# THE DEALER

Whether you're an experienced leader or a novice taking on your first challenge, new groups can create a sense of panic. The talent of the chairperson is either the glue that keeps things together or the broken piece that keeps things from fitting quite right. The leader defines the meeting: is it a process or merely an event? The Chairperson is the role model for group attitudes and enthusiasm. DIRECTION, PREPARATION, PARTICIPATION AND ACTION, all begin with the Chair.

Leadership is more than mechanical execution of tasks. Results are achieved through the stimulation of minds, not the delegation and assignment of responsibilities. Leaders that inspire results are attuned to the group and its needs and the individuals and their needs. Leaders know when to push, when to allow space and when to force conclusions; they *absorb* the group and its feel.

***The Leader Names the Game.*** As the focal point for direction, the leader provides the spark that fuels the group. It's the leader who convinces the group to try and try again when progress is slow or difficult. It's the leader who "cheers" to success.

The tone and organization of the group are defined by the Chair. When questions arise, it's the Chair who helps to direct the response. Explaining the rules, prioritizing the issues, focusing the group and activating the exchange are all responsibilities that help to assure that the Name of the Game is fully understood.

***The Leader is Ready for the Deal.*** The Chairperson assumes primary responsibility for anticipating discussion and identifying the needs of the group. It's the Chairperson who makes sure that everyone knows what to expect – and what's expected of them. Good preparation begins with leaders who plan well and communicate thoroughly.

***The Leader Deals Everybody in.*** The Chairperson markets fairness and objectivity. Equity within the group begins with leadership that is impartial and fair – everyone is treated with respect and consideration is shown for the needs and values of others. Good leaders earn the respect of the group through the respect that they show toward others.

Leaders who inspire great contributions capture the attention of the group and diligently pursue progress. They know when to call for a break and when to push on. They're skilled at drawing out minority opinions and work hard to maintain appropriate balance within the group. Good leaders are good listeners.

***Leaders Win the Game.*** The leader inspires action after the meeting is over. The successful Chair is able to coach, nudge and guide the group toward the goal. When issues get lost or enthusiasm for the job dwindles, the leader provides encouragement and renewed commitment to move on toward completion. By understanding both the capacities and the limitations of the group, the skillful Chair strikes a balance between overwhelming demands and boring assignments. The best leaders win the game because of the energy they generate, not the enthusiasm they drain.

## LEARNING TO SHUFFLE

Leadership is perfected with practice. The key is to understand the responsibility and what it means, while maintaining the courage to "just do it." Most new chairpersons will find that overwhelming support resides within their groups: members have a vested interest in helping to produce an effective meeting. Leaders can tap this resource by simply saying "help . . . " – "time out . . . " – "I need . . ." – "could you . . ." – Logically, experience helps to develop skill and personalize the application.

Leading is a talent that is tuned over time.  To develop the skill, begin by watching groups in operation – what signals communicate the tone, what behaviors indicate stalls, and what cues transmit overload?  What are the common strengths of the chair?

Fine-tuning the talent begins with self-knowledge.  What kind of leader would you make?  How do you measure up?  Where do you need to grow, where do you shine?  The best Chairpersons are in a state of constant training.  Systematic self-development allows for continual progress.  Improvement is always possible; there's something to be learned from the greatest of successes as well as the most disastrous of catastrophes.

To become the best that you can be:

1. KNOW YOURSELF.  Acknowledge your strengths and weaknesses.  Take time for reflection and honest assessment of your skills.  Make self-evaluation a habit.

2. SET GOALS.  Where would you like to be?  In exact terms, what does it look like?  Make your objectives specific.

3. DEVELOP A PLAN.  Identify what will be needed to achieve your goals.  List your needs, the help you'll rely on and what specifically you can and will do.

4. LOOK FOR MENTORS AND ROLE MODELS.  Whom do you respect?  Whose style would you like to emulate?  Talk to those who personify your ideals.  Find out what it takes to "make it."  What approaches do others use for the meetings they

lead?  Volunteer to co-chair with one of your role models and assist the "master at work."

5. PERFECT YOUR ORGANIZATION.  Are you satisfied with your ability to keep things under control or are you always one step away from chaos?  Do you have it together or are you always wondering where they put it?  Who are the most organized people you know?  How do they do it?  Find out.

6. BECOME, NEVER BE.  Place yourself in a state of perpetual improvement.  Observe groups in action: what works and what doesn't work?  What would you do differently?  Talk to others.  What would they do differently?

7. PRACTICE.  Lead as many groups as you can.  Try helping with Chairperson responsibilities; volunteer to co-chair with an experienced mentor; suggest rotating the chair for standing groups. "Just do it."

## DEALING THE CARDS

From planning the first meeting to tracking assignments, the chairperson is busy. Meetings begin as soon as the idea to meet is formed and end only after the last decision has been implemented.  Making the commitment to assume the responsibility can be "awesome."

Organization is the key to success. Organization supports delegation and frees the leader to lead; it allows the chairperson to orchestrate as it all comes together, rather than agonize because nothing seems to be getting done. Meeting arrangements can be managed with checklists; minutes can be standardized and delegated. Organized agendas clearly indicate who will assume the responsibility for leading discussion as well as what is expected of members before the meeting. From pre-meeting chores to evaluation of the meeting and its members, organization helps to make sure that it all gets done. (For examples of just how such organization can be accomplished, see "Tools of the Trade," beginning on page 100.)

The task of superchair *can* be delegated and achieved. By standardizing the routine tasks like pre-meeting communications, agendas and meeting minutes, time and energies can be devoted to those responsibilities that require the attention of the leader. Remember: being responsible doesn't mean doing everything yourself. Being responsible *does* mean making sure that everything gets done.

*"When the greatest of leaders has finished his work, the people will say they did it themselves." (Lao Tsu)*

# IN SUMMARY

TO LEARN TO SHUFFLE:

1.  Know yourself
2.  Set goals
3.  Develop a plan
4.  Look for mentors and role models
5.  Perfect your organization
6.  Become, never be
7.  Practice

**Poker Faces**

CHAPTER **5**

# POKER FACES

In spite of careful selection, every meeting will not be a perfect blend of peace and harmony. Whether your character list includes the bold and boisterous or the meek and mild, the human factor *will* influence the outcome of the meeting. Because meetings are people, the personalities and attitudes of the participants can and do influence the outcome of the game. Solutions can disappear as they form because someone's personality is too domineering, too passive, too patronizing, or too selfish.

Eliminating differences is both unnecessary and undesirable. Differences of opinion are a healthy part of the meeting process. Yet, striking a balance is critical to effectiveness: all views and sides of the issue need to be heard. The force of one  individual or view should not obliterate other members or other opinions. Protecting differences, while at the same time smoothing conflict, can be an interesting, if not difficult, challenge for the average chairperson.

Every situation demands its own solution. However, there are a few principles that can often help in the development, management, or improvement of any meeting. The "Character Control Code:"

1. TWO OF A KIND BEATS AN ODD PAIR:  GET TO AGREEMENT.

2. PLAY BY THE RULES:  PROTECT FAIR PLAY.

3. KEEP YOUR MIND ON THE CARDS:  BY-PASS THE DETOURS.

4. IT'S A FRIENDLY GAME:  CONTAIN THE COMPETITION.

5. PUT YOUR CARDS ON THE TABLE:  ADJUST THE ATTITUDES.

## GET TO AGREEMENT

The glow of success can often soften the negative impact of dispute.  It's a well known fact that agreement reinforces a persuasive argument.  When opposition is expected, it's best to look for the "yes" before stimulating the "no."  To get to agreement:

- POINT OUT SIMILARITIES.  Underscore points of agreement between groups and individuals or yourself and others:

    "I know both of you would agree that. . ."
    "Like you, I believe that . . . "
    "I agree. ____________ is important."

- USE COMPARISONS.  Gain support by using comparisons to other groups, organizations that have approval in the eyes of the audience/individual:

    "This survey from XYZ organization shows that our ________ is very similar.  Ours is ______ , theirs ______ ."
    "We've conferred with Dept/Individual X for guidance in development of this proposal.  Their input has been invaluable."

- YES ITEMS FIRST.  Arrange the agenda such that positive agenda items, sure to get agreement, precede those that predict conflict or livelier discussion.

## PROTECT FAIR PLAY

Whether faced with explosive issues or routine matters, a sense of "fair play" is critical to meeting success. Impartiality helps to overcome negative and defensive attitudes and sets the stage for objective discussion of the issues. Fairness assures that the best possible decisions can be made. To create fair play:

- FOCUS ON FACTS. What are the observable truths?
  "That's an interesting observation."
  "Could you research that point so that we are better apprised of the facts?"
  "The data show. . . ."

- INVITE OPPOSITION. Make sure that all sides of the issue/proposal are aired.
  "Why don't we invite __________ to make sure that we clearly understand this issue from all sides."
  "Have we considered everyone who will be affected by this decision?"

- CONTAIN THE DOMINANT. Try to give others equal air time:
  "Thanks for your opinions, Ralph. Perhaps we could hear from someone else now."
  "Rachel, I know that you have feelings about this. Do you have any insights to share?"

- LIMIT DISCUSSION. Contain verbose or out of control speakers.

  "We have roughly five minutes left for discussion before we make a decision."

- EXPAND DISCUSSION. Assure that all issues can be completely presented; schedule discussion across several meetings if necessary to complete discussion.

  "We're clearly running out of time to reach a conclusion. What remains to be discussed? How much time do we need? When can/should we do it?"

- ADD MEMBERS. Balance opinion and assure that absent or missing viewpoints are adequately represented.

- BE CONSISTENT. Make sure that rules of the group are equally applied to all.

## BY-PASS THE DETOURS

Hidden agendas, personal interests, and egocentricity – can all get in the way of forward movement. Unfortunately, some groups wander according to the purposes of their members, not the goals of the group. Focusing on the issues and not the personalities is often a major challenge. To by-pass the detours:

- **Agree to the Destination.** What are the real limits and reasonable expectations of the group?
  "What would you like to see done?"
  "Is this within the scope of this group?"
  "Our mission is. . ."

- **Nudge Toward the Goal.** Remind that the discussion seems to be wandering from the goal or the topic:
  "We seem to have strayed from our objective/topic."
  "How is it that this relates to our discussion?"

- **Decide on Priorities.** Is this the best use of the group's time right now? Make sure that the most important issues are being addressed first.

- **Respond to the Issues.** Is it the issues you're responding to or the personalities? Focus on logic and fact, not emotion.

## Contain the Competition

Competition and control issues frequently disrupt the happy glow of the conference room. Whether long-standing disputes or new wounds, competitive behavior can get in the way of creative solutions. To contain the competition:

- CULTIVATE CAMARADERIE. It *is* all for one and one for all! Promote activities that require total team, avoid endorsing competitions that exacerbate existing conflicts.

- PROMOTE SENSITIVITY. Help groups and individuals to understand one another better.

- LIGHTEN THE MOOD. Have a little fun! Learning to share a laugh together helps to soften competitive edges.

- SHARE RESPONSIBILITIES. Get competitors to work together in a cooperative situation. Sharing the responsibility promotes ownership and helps to balance negative attitudes and opinions.

## ADJUST THE ATTITUDES

*"We tried to do that once before."*
*"It'll never work."*
*"This is a waste of time."*
*"Nobody ever listens anyway."*

What influence do these attitudes have on your meetings? Attitudes, the mind-sets that we wear into the room like hats, can control a meeting. These mind-monsters can take over the agenda and dismantle the purpose. The mentality of the group can destroy direction and obliterate positive accomplishments. Attitudes that obstruct logical discussion ruin results.

For groups that must continue to meet, some attempt must be made to contain, if not change, those attitudes that are disrupting the meeting process. For groups that will not be convening again, destructive attitudes can defeat the purpose of the meeting and waste everyone's time. To adjust the attitudes:

- FACE THE FACTS. Find or make an opportunity to talk in private with the individual(s) involved. If necessary, this can be accomplished by taking a short break or by making arrangements for a between meeting discussion. Identify the issues; what are the attitudes, why do they exist? What facts/actions support the attitudes?

- MAKE A PACT. What facts/actions will change the attitude? Agree to a specific description of "proof." Develop a plan to make it happen.

- CALL A TRUCE. Recognize that past behaviors and perceptions cannot be changed. Agree to a period of neutrality, during which new history can be made. Commit to a philosophy that says "from this point forward."

- GO PUBLIC? Examine the extent to which this attitude has affected the entire group. Plan agenda time to execute a "truce" with everyone.

# THE PERFECT COMBINATION . . .

Meetings are people.  Eliminating differences is not only impossible, it's undesirable.  The Characters in the chairs become a problem only when they're allowed to interfere with group process.  When personalities and destructive behaviors get in the way of goal attainment, it's time to take action.

The wise leader knows when control is needed and when exploration would be more appropriate.  Fair play and respect for others are critical to the "Character Control" process.  Remember:  The objective is not to remove attitudes and personalities from meetings; the objective is to assure that meetings are spiced with the challenge and excitement of reality, not devoured by individuals or their attitudes.

*Viva la Difference!*

# IN SUMMARY

THE CHARACTER CONTROL CODE:
1.  *Two of a kind beats an odd pair:  Get to agreement*
    * Point out similarities
    * Use comparisons
    * Yes items first

2.  *Play by the rules:  Protect fair play*
    * Focus on facts
    * Invite opposition
    * Contain the dominant
    * Limit discussion
    * Expand discussion
    * Add members
    * Subtract members
    * Be consistent

3.  *Keep your mind on the cards:  By-pass the detours*
    * Agree to the destination
    * Nudge toward the goal
    * Decide on priorities
    * Respond to the issues

4.  *It's a friendly Game:  Contain the competition*
    * Cultivate camaraderie
    * Promote sensitivity
    * Lighten the mood
    * Share responsibilities

5.  *Put Your cards on the Table:  Adjust the attitudes*
    * Face the facts
    * Make a pact
    * Call a truce
    * Go public:  Discuss the problem with the group

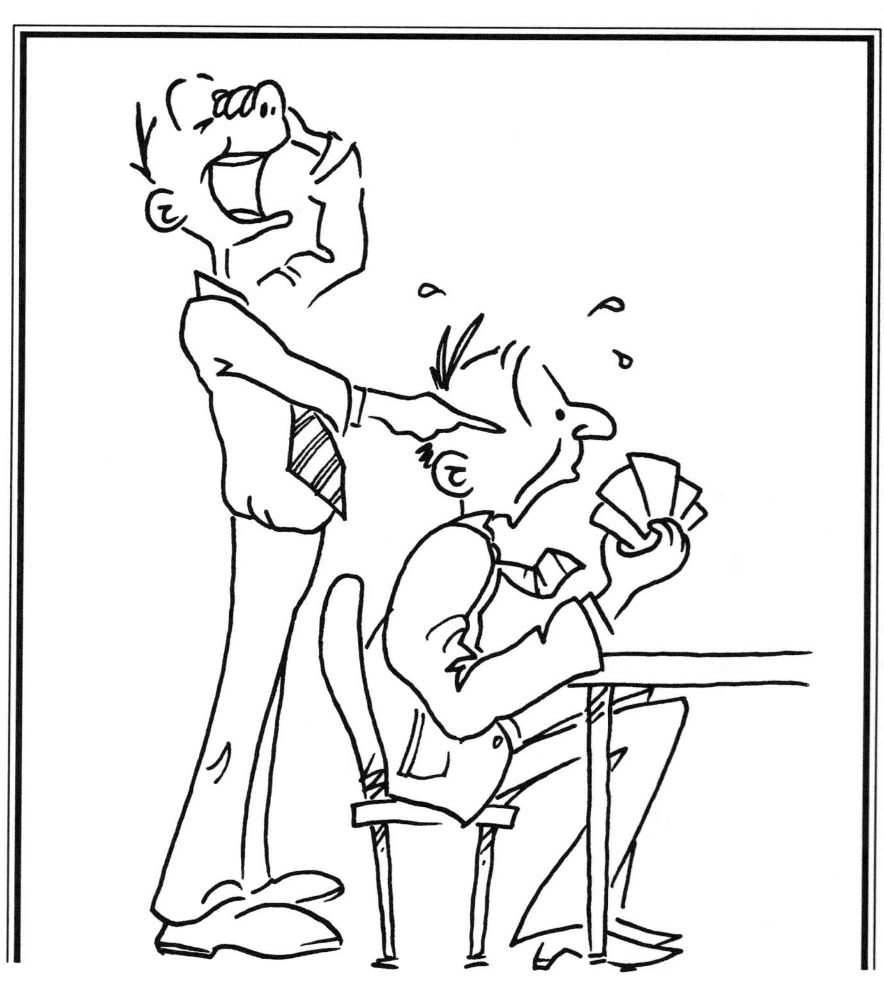

**The Losing Hand**

CHAPTER 6

# The Losing Hand

Meetings can exhaust as well as inspire; those that stop producing results are a drain. They waste time and destroy motivation. Worse still, they rob us of productive opportunities: they cost us money. Hours wasted in fruitless meetings are expensive.

Characteristics of meetings that are in trouble are often similar. Results are delayed or non-existent, members are frequently absent or show obvious disinterest. The Losing Hand is usually missing one or more of the ACES, direction, preparation, participation or action. The Losing Hand is not structured for success.

Direction is the framework that guides the meeting. Without the guidance of a clear purpose statement and skilled leadership, meetings flounder. Lack of direction shows. When the purpose is not shared or is poorly understood, members set their own goals. If this happens, the productivity of the group is reliant on the natural organization of the members. The primary purpose of the group becomes unimportant to most members; the meeting becomes an end in itself.

LOSING HANDS are characterized by disorganization. Members of the group rarely know what to expect or what's expected of them. Because no attempts are made to plan agenda time, time frequently runs out before all agenda items have been discussed. The exact length of the meeting is usually unknown. "It depends" is the general rule. Communication is inconsistent and unreliable.

When it's clear that you have a LOSING HAND, it's time to take stock before the losses mount up.

## WHEN TO HOLD 'EM

The only reason to save a dying meeting is because the purpose to be achieved is of high priority and great importance. Yet, a meeting that is showing signs of trouble is not achieving its purpose. If the purpose is important and the results are questionable, take time out. Put the meeting on the agenda. Discuss the problems; use the group to consider the best way to reach the goals.

Where's the problem?  Is it the way that the meeting is structured or the way that it's led?  Is it the composition of personalities or the competition among members?  What keeps this important purpose from being achieved?  Assessment often sparks new life for a group that's stumped or hopelessly out of balance.  An adjustment in the players, the dealer or the game itself is often just what's needed for success.

## THE GAME

There are some meetings with vital purposes that are simply not structured for action.  "The Game" is poorly defined or badly organized; expectations are vague; results, questionable.  When the structure critical for success is either absent or weak, even the most important meeting becomes a liability.  The essential structure begins with the Aces:  Direction, preparation, participation and action.

Are you playing with a full deck?  Are any of the ACES missing?  How does this "hand" compare to the WINNING HAND?  Sometimes all that's needed is an accurate diagnosis of the problem.  What specific areas need improvement?  How does the group see the problem?  Are the right tools available to assure that all aspects of the meeting process are used?  Spark new life – find the Aces.

***Direction:*** Start with the basics. Make sure that there is common understanding and commitment to the purpose. Do members know the purpose? Have they had opportunity to discuss it? Do they grasp its importance? Is the purpose too broad in scope? Too narrow to stimulate results? For standing committees, groups that go on year after year, the purpose should evolve with the needs in the environment. Groups that fail to update their purpose may find that the right group is meeting about the wrong things.

Good direction is communicated by expectations that support the purpose and help to move the group forward. Reviewing the game includes examining the rules. What standards for operation exist? Are they too loose or too tight? Is everyone clear about what's expected? Have communication channels been defined? Is exchange reliable and predictable?

When it's time to unify direction:

- REGROUP. Hold a session dedicated to a review of the purpose of the meeting. Develop a plan for its communication and attainment. Commit to its achievement.

- REPORT. Include routine reports regarding progress toward goal attainment as a normal part of operation. Add the meeting to the agenda at routine intervals.

- INSPIRE. Fuel renewed commitment to the purpose with discussions about the purpose, its importance and progress that has been made.

- REORGANIZE.  For meetings that are one in a series or part of an ongoing committee, the routine tasks needed for meeting effectiveness can get lost. Reorganizing – "starting over" – helps to reestablish direction and improve the effectiveness of the meeting management.  Reorganization should always include a review of who's doing what as well as what needs to be done.

- AGREE.  Discuss meeting responsibilities with the group.  Agree and commit to the "Rules of the Game."

- FOCUS.  Distractions, whether global or individual, make even the best of groups dysfunctional. Distractions can often be lessened by placing more attention on the "creature comforts" in the room - lighting, temperature control and seating arrangements.  Minimizing the environmental distractions frequently helps to focus the group and get it back on track.

***Preparation:***  The most impressive meetings are those in which discussion occurs naturally and spontaneously; those in which members know what they're talking about and forward progress occurs easily and often.  Impressive meetings demand great preparation.

When preparation is missing, those issues that require time for thought get none.  Meetings become less effective and results come either slowly or not at all. When the preparation for your meeting needs a tonic, try one of these:

- STANDARDIZE.  Set standards for agenda content and distribution so that pre-meeting information is consistent in content and in quality.

- COMMUNICATE.  Get back to basics.  Reinforce the importance of communication.  Look for ways that inadequate communication may be starving preparation.  Enhance preparation and build on results by clearly identifying pre-meeting responsibilities.

- SHARE.  Schedule a special session devoted only to preparation activities.  Use the group spirit to make preparation a cooperative chore.  Encourage individuals to share personal strategies for overcoming procrastination.

***Participation:***  Good team dialogue begins with members who are committed to fair and open participation.  When equity within the meeting room is threatened, the "dialogue that promotes understanding" can't occur.  Imbalance can turn a valued group into a pile of dead issues.  To revitalize participation:

- RESCHEDULE.  Consider rescheduling the meeting to a day, time or place that holds fewer distractions.  Adjust the frequency of meetings to improve productivity, to provide greater continuity, to allow more time for between meeting work – or simply to enhance the convenience for members.  Capture an extra ten minutes to get people there on time:  change the meeting time from *on* the hour to ten minutes *after* the hour.

- ADJUST.  Adjust the meeting length so that the energy of the group is maximized.  For some groups this will mean longer meetings, for others shorter.

- ELIMINATE.  For those members who are always "in touch" with their world via beeper or telephone, interruptions can cause nearly terminal disruption to a meeting.  Suggest that a secretary assume responsibility for handling both during the meeting.  Limit disruptions to the true emergency only.

***Action:***  Making the investment requires commitment.  When meetings go on and on and nothing ever changes, members get discouraged.  Those who have been subdued by inertia are usually less than enthusiastic participants.  Apathy has its seeds in procrastination and obstructed productivity.  When the results are delayed:

- REFLECT.  Take time out for reflection.  What is it that seems to be stifling progress?  What specific actions can be taken to circumvent or plow through the barriers?

- RE-EVALUATE.  Is the problem the group or the goal?  Evaluate the goal.  When progress can't be achieved, it may be because the goal is unrealistic or impractical.  Examine the group.  Does the mix of personalities and skill promote effective action? What skill, power, chemistry would improve the probability of success?

- REGROUP. Is this noise or music? Have all of the actions necessary for success been considered? Are the right people working on the right things? Regroup. Decide how to rearrange so that productivity increases.

- COMMIT. Discuss the progress (or lack thereof!) with the group. Decide what factors contribute to group procrastination and ineffectiveness. Create and commit to a plan for overcoming inertia.

## THE DEALER

Confronting and correcting a leadership problem can be a difficult and delicate process. If you're the leader, it's not always easy to learn that you may be part of the problem. Most leaders truly want to be effective; it's just not always possible. Other commitments or urgent issues may present unreasonable distractions; or it may simply be the "wrong chemistry" – the wrong group at the wrong time.

Leadership problems are noticed. Sometimes there's a definite "Kill the King" urge; other times, no one discusses "it," but everyone "knows." Groups may feel that the Chair stifles dialogue or that the Leader controls rather than facilitates discussions. The Leader's tone and mood may quiet the group and dampen discussion.  The Leader's discomfort may disquiet the group.

Leadership is salvageable when:  1)  the leader recognizes the problem, 2) the leader *wants to* make adjustments needed, and 3)  changes needed can be accomplished within a reasonable length of time.  When the decision has been made to tune rather than prune the leadership, the ideas that follow may be helpful starting points.

***For Group Members:***  Group members who decide to tackle the leadership of the group are often seen as mutineers rather than Good Samaritans.  It's important to remember that you are the only person you can control enough to change.  Groups that are frustrated with a less than effective leader can benefit most by trying to change those things within their immediate command:  themselves and the way that they relate to the leader and the meeting.

- ENCOURAGE.  Cheering is always more helpful than jeering.  Leadership can be improved the most when an air of support rather than accusation exists.  Direct feedback and positive encouragement set the stage for team work.  Teamwork creates better results.

- ASSIST.  The responsibilities of the Chair can be overwhelming.  Sometimes finding ways to make the job more manageable increases the effectiveness of the leader dramatically.  Try using a co-chair to share the responsibilities or find a secretary to assist with organization. Get group members to alternate the "assistant" responsibilities.

- ROTATE. When the responsibilities of leading the group are overwhelming or simply too much for one person to manage, try rotating the Chairperson responsibilities among all members. In addition to improving the manageability of the responsibilities, rotation also develops empathy and group support for the role. Rotation works best, of course, for those groups whose existence is part of routine operations.

- COOPERATE. When the leadership void is filled by the group, members often choose to ignore the "Rules of the Game." When this happens, chaos emerges. Support a shaky chair by knowing and doing your job.

***For the Chairperson:*** It takes courage to notice and admit one's own problems. Yet, problems aren't resolved without recognition. When the leader is interested in serious improvement, a strict regime of self-development is in order:

- SHARE. Discuss your meetings with those who attend them. The strength of the informal group can often help the Chair to get a more complete picture of the meeting dynamics. By increasing the leader's understanding of the group, "easy" solutions can frequently be found.

- COLLABORATE.  Collaborate with those who chair other meetings.  Find out what works in their meetings.  Pool resources to help one another.  Exchange ideas for running better and more effective meetings.

- TRAIN.  A good coach is a great asset for any leader and is essential for those leaders who are struggling with problems.  Leaders who are fortunate enough to discover and recognize their need for help often benefit from a mentor who can teach new skills and help polish old tricks.

- LEARN.  Leadership seminars, meetings, one-on-one discussion, reading: we all know the ways that information is shared.  Those interested in self-development will want to make sure that the information exchange provides true learning: what did I gain from this experience?  How and when can I apply it?

- EVALUATE.  Routine self-evaluations are an excellent source of instant, personal and direct feedback.  Incorporate reflection into your routine; make evaluations a priority.

- PLAN.  What's your goal?  How do you want to change?  What do you want to learn?  Define your plan in simple and direct terms.  Make it practical. Use it.

Leadership problems are felt by the Chairperson. Leading the play is a big responsibility; it's one that most don't take lightly. For many, the fact that this group "doesn't work" equates to failure. It's frustrating. Emotions can range from hurt to anger. The leader may be quick to assume all of the blame ("I must be a bad leader . . .") or angrily denying any responsibility ("Nobody cooperated . . .") Understanding this perspective is critical when salvage is not possible or desirable, when balance must be restored by changing the Chair.

Approaching the situation directly and objectively focuses the attention on the needs of the group and not the deficits of the leader. "Giving up" need not be seen in negative terms: relief often provides an opportunity to be more effective with other groups or with other projects. When the match is not right, it's not right. "Force fitting" doesn't always work. Remember: the objective is to achieve the best results in the most efficient amount of time. *Finding* the right person is often just as important as *being* the right person.

## THE PLAYERS

Participation is the heart of the meeting; the players are the heart of participation. Meetings are held for exchange, for dialogue not monologue. When the group is "dead," the purpose of the meeting is defeated. It may be just "one of those days," it may be a chronic problem person or a simple imbalance in the group. Whatever the cause, the first step is identification.

***The Bad Day:*** Even the best groups aren't always functioning at optimum speed. Ho-hum days produce ho-hum results. When discussion is falling flat and leading turns into pulling, the signs are clearly pointing to a "bad day." The suggestions that follow may help to stimulate the enthusiasm that's missing:

- ENERGIZE. Take an energy break: use the big muscles to send a spark back to the brain. Breaks are a great way to step back, refocus and re-energize the group. Use break times as they're needed, not "on schedule."

- PLAY. Lighten the mood; change the tone. Tell a joke; ask the group to share their jokes. Take a laugh break to loosen things up.

- STIMULATE. Use brain teasers and other mental exercises to stimulate creativity. Get the group contributing easily about a non-threatening topic before tackling the "real biggy."

- ADJOURN. When nothing seems to work, it may be time to adjourn. The better use of time may be to dismiss the group and regroup for another day. If adjournment is the option selected, make the development of a plan for success "next time" the last task for the day.

***The Uneven Balance:*** Strong opinions, potent personalities and intense individuals can all contribute to imbalances. When either power or opinion are out of balance, fair discussion is jeopardized.  Disturbances are evident in who talks as well as in who only listens.  The dynamics of *why* someone chooses not to contribute are often significant.  Good participation depends on good balance.  To promote balance:

- COACH.  Talk to members between meetings; find out how they feel about issues.  Give direct feedback regarding behaviors that are detrimental to group progress; recognize actions that support forward movement.  Help each member understand how they can help to shape the whole.

- LISTEN.  Listen to what the group is saying – observe the dynamics.  Listen and learn how to draw out the quiet, protect the minority, silence the talkative, challenge the creative.

- EQUALIZE.  Examine the mix of the group.  Do any groups or individuals overpower others?  Is it possible to make changes?  Would adding members help to balance power or opinion?  Is membership reduction appropriate?

***The Problem Person:***  Personality clashes, negative attitudes, and power struggles can threaten to undo the success of any meeting.  Members who cannot focus on the objectives, who refuse to make the effort necessary to participate or who obstruct progress in other ways are a detriment to the group.  When it's obvious that some*one* is becoming a menace to the productivity of the group:

- REINFORCE THE RULES. Reinforce the "Rules of the Game" with all members. Make sure that everyone understands how to make the investment worthwhile. Take care to assure that no individual or group is getting preferential treatment and that all members understand exactly what's expected and why.

- CONFRONT THE BEHAVIOR. When destructive behaviors are allowed to continue unchecked, the morale of the group can often be destroyed. Even those members who are committed to action, can adopt a "Why try?" attitude. It's important, therefore, to identify the problem person and confront the behavior directly. Make arrangements to talk outside of the meeting. Try to determine why the behavior exists, and, more importantly, what can be done to change it. Make sure that the problem person understands the effect of their behavior on the group and how it is that they're expected to change.

- MAKE A CHANGE. If allowed to persist unchecked, disruptions can become terminal. When all signs point to terminal disruption, removal of members from the group should be considered. Eliminating members can serve many purposes: it can help create consistent attendance, speed progress and even improve the functioning of other group members.

     The actual removal of a member, however, can be both a difficult decision and a potential problem. Yet, the objective is to improve the productivity of the meeting, not to maintain membership that is either destructive or no longer helpful for the issues at hand.

- ENCOURAGE SELF-EVALUATION.  As with other difficulties, the best way to avoid a problem is often to prevent it.  When routine opportunities for personal self-evaluations are provided, each person understands how they are or are not helping to move the group forward.  When evaluations are a matter of routine, individuals don't feel singled out. – And, it's easier for those who may have outserved their useful purpose to the group to self-identify and move on to other projects.

***The Problem Group:***  Try as we might, there are some groups that just won't work.  Every day feels like a "bad day" – energy is low, progress is slow.  When the group is not producing and it's obviously not just a bad day, it's time to look for an infusion.  To revitalize the team:

- EXAMINE THE DYNAMICS.  What's working within the group?  What's not working?  Why is it that this group seems to be struggling so hard?  Is it because of the number of members or the type of personalities involved?  If possible try to identify and pinpoint the reason for the dysfunction.

- REVISE THE GROUP.  Review member selection as compared to the purpose of the group.  Does member selection relate to and support the purpose?    Make recommendations regarding changes needed for the appointment of future groups or the next selection of this group.

Consider the size of the group.   Given the purpose and the number of people that it affects, should the group be larger or smaller?  Document recommendations so that they can be incorporated in the future.  If at all possible, adjust group size immediately.

- REJUVENATE FOR NEW IDEAS.   Are new ideas and fresh perspectives needed?   Consider adding individuals who have knowledge or experience that would add a helpful dimension to the group.

## WHEN TO FOLD 'EM

When meetings that are "finished" aren't over, everybody loses.   Salvage may not always be either reasonable or desirable.  If the purpose is gone, it's time to adjourn.   Meetings should be adjourned and not reconvened when the mission has either been attained or lost.

THE MISSION IS ACCOMPLISHED when the purpose of the group has been realized.  Specifically, the results produced have satisfied the goals of the group; all goals have been reached.

THE MISSION IS LOST when the purpose of the group has been removed or is no longer a priority, when the drive toward the goal disappears.  The mission is in danger if results are not being achieved.   In rapidly changing times, there are many events that can place a mission in limbo.  New priorities, changes in the environment, urgent problems – all can jeopardize the mission.  When results are not evident, start searching for the mission of the group; it may have been lost.

## CASHING IN THE CHIPS

*"When group members have time to reflect, they can see more clearly what is essential in themselves and others."* (Lao Tzu)

Whether you're folding this meeting because the mission has been accomplished or because your attempts at revival failed, you *will* want to look at what you've won or lost from this experience.  Even "bad" meetings can be turned into winners.

Time is a valuable resource.  Allowing ourselves to be "drawn into" meetings can have a disastrous effect on our time management.  It's critical that we review what it is that we're gaining or losing.  Your next investment benefits directly from the review of this experience.  What did *you* win?

- UNDERSTANDING.  Did your direct involvement replace "they" with "we?"  Every meeting offers the opportunity to learn more about others and how issues affect them.  The interaction of the meeting helps to create a common first-hand experience.  Turn yours into one that provides an appreciation for the issues that you can share with others.

Do you have a better understanding of your role within a group?  What strengths do you have? Where do you need development?  What do you have to offer others?

- PERSPECTIVE.  Interaction provides a chance to see issues from another perspective.  What sides of the issue did this meeting bring into focus for you? Did it help to clarify reality and balance biases?

- COMMITMENT.  Did you get involved?  Did the experience help to personalize decisions that were made?  Do you feel ownership for the results?  If not, why not?  What would need to change in future groups?

- ACTION.  What will you do?  Will you make an effort to change or help others to change as a result of this meeting?  If this meeting didn't work, what will you do to make the next investment a better investment?

Become the best that you can be.  Make the commitment to make even the not-so-good pay off. Take time for reflection.  Let the hand that you "fold" become the inspiration that makes your next hand a WINNING HAND.

*Perfect the Process!*

# IN SUMMARY

TO SALVAGE A LOSING HAND:

1. *Verify the direction of the game*
   - Regroup around the purpose
   - Report progress
   - Inspire commitment
   - Reorganize for effectiveness
   - Agree to "Rules of the Game"
   - Focus the group

2. *Feed preparation for the game*
   - Standardize agendas
   - Communicate preparation expectations
   - Share strategies for improvement

3. *Activate participation in the game*
   - Reschedule for productivity
   - Adjust the length to capture more energy
   - Eliminate distractions

4. *Inspire action, overcome inertia*
   - Reflect on the barriers
   - Re-evaluate the goal and the group
   - Regroup to increase productivity
   - Commit to action

SUMMARY CONT'D.

5. *Enlist member support to develop the leader*
   - Offer encouragement
   - Assist with responsibilities
   - Rotate the leadership
   - Cooperate by following the rules

6. *Perfect the leadership*
   - Share perspectives
   - Collaborate with other Chairpersons
   - Find a coach and train
   - Look for learning opportunities
   - Evaluate personal progress
   - Plan for self-development

7. *Invigorate the group:  Attack the bad day*
   - Take an energy break
   - Lighten the mood
   - Stimulate the minds
   - Adjourn  .

8. *Promote balance*
   - Coach for success.
   - Listen to the group
   - Equalize the membership

9. *Check the problem person*
   - Reinforce the rules
   - Confront the behavior
   - Make a change
   - Encourage self-evaluation

SUMMARY CONT'D.

10. *Remodel the problem group*
    • Examine the dynamics
    • Revise the group
    • Rejuvenate for new ideas

11. *Know when to fold 'em*
    • When the mission is accomplished
    • When the mission is lost

The Final Score

**CHAPTER 7**

# THE FINAL SCORE

Board meeting or task force – standing committee, ad hoc project, educational session – What form do your meetings take? Regardless of purpose, the bottom line for any meeting is: *what kind of results at what cost?* Was this a good investment? How much time, money and attention were required? What was put aside, what opportunities were missed because of resources that were exhausted? Was the price worth the payoff?

The best meetings achieve results: benefits that can be measured directly – problems solved, ideas implemented, plans made. They create spirit and momentum that extends beyond the meeting room; productive groups *care* about results. They make a difference. The best meetings are worth the investment.

How do *you* decide which meetings to attend, which groups to join? Based on your friendship with the Chair? Because you know lots of people who will be there? Because it's a pet project of one of your special friends? Or is it be because you're simply tired of being badgered?

The choices we make *are* important. From the clothes we buy to the careers we consider, we are presented with more options for more aspects of our lives than we can digest. We are literally drowning in choice. Yet choose we must; "not to decide is to decide." In this world of alternatives, it takes diligent resource management to maintain the energy, enthusiasm and time to take advantage of the really great opportunities.

Making the commitment to meet is a big decision, one that requires careful consideration of the investment. Avoid wasting time in meetings that aren't producing results. Pick the best meetings, the *right* meetings. When considering your next decision, play like a pro:

1. BET ON THE ACES. The ACES are a part of every WINNING HAND. Look for direction, preparation, participation and action.

2. PLAY BY THE RULES. Whether dealer or player, study your role. Learn how to get the most out of the time that you invest.

3. PUT YOUR CHIPS ON YOUR STRONG SUITS. It's critical that each person, leader or player, have intimate knowledge of their own strengths and weaknesses. Make the choices that capitalize on your talent.

3. KNOW WHEN TO FOLD 'EM. What's the bottom line? Has the purpose been achieved, is the mission alive? When it's over, adjourn.

## PLACE YOUR BETS

Meetings can pose an insidious threat to the individual and the organization; meeting "creep" can be a terminal disease, eating holes in productivity, destroying the time needed for the new challenge or the exciting opportunity. The "dead" group can be a dangerous waste of time.

Agreeing to meet without understanding the purpose and the investment can be disastrous. Remember: productive meetings have purpose statements that present a precise vision of the desired outcome. Expectations from participants before, during and after the meeting are clearly communicated; timetables and commitment are explicit. Action is guaranteed. Winners know how to hold 'em.

Individuals and organizations should add it up *before* making the commitment. Is the investment worth the payoff? What will be gained, what will be lost through this meeting? Is this a priority? Winners know when to fold 'em.

The cards are in your hands. What is the best investment of your time? Are you willing to make the investment necessary to assure success?

*It's Your Deal!!!*

# REFERENCES

Cleveland, Harland. *The Knowledge Executive: Leadership in an Information Society.* New York: Truman Tulley Books. E.P Dutton., 1989.

DePree, Max. *Leadership is an Art.* Lansing, Michigan: Michigan State University Press, 1987.

Heider, John. *The Tao of Leadership: Leadership Strategies for a New Age.* New York: Bantom Books, 1985.

Neis, Marlys E. and Ruth T. Kingdon. *Leadership in Transition: A Practical Guide to Shared Governance.* Schaumburg, Illinois: NOVA I, Ltd., 1990.

Tools of the Trade

# Tools of the Trade

<table><tr><td colspan="2" align="center">OUR MEETING</td></tr></table>

PURPOSE: ______________________________________________

CHAIRPERSON: _________________________________ PHONE: ____________

START DATE: __________________________________ END DATE: __________

LOCATION: ❏ DIRECTIONS ATTACHED   ❏ TBA   ❏ OTHER __________________

LENGTH OF EACH MTG: _________________

ESTIMATED # OF MEETINGS: _____________

EXPECTATIONS:   ❏ SEE ATTACHED        ❏ AS DISCUSSED

<table><tr><td colspan="2" align="center">THE MEMBERSHIP</td></tr><tr><td align="center">NAME/DEPARTMENT</td><td align="center">PHONE/EXT.</td></tr></table>

# PRE-MEETING CHECKLIST

MEETING: ________________________________________  DATE: ________________

| COMMUNICATIONS | | ARRANGEMENTS | | |
| --- | --- | --- | --- | --- |
| | [✓] | ITEM | CONTACT | ✓ |
| Agenda | | Rm. Reservation | | |
| Pre-meeting Memos | | Seating Arrangements | | |
| | | A.V. Equipment | | |
| | | Microphone | | |
| | | Food/Refreshments | | |
| CALLS | | OTHER — Flipchart | | |
| | | Markers | | |
| | | | | |
| | | | | |
| | | | | |

| ASSIGNMENTS | | | SUPPORT MATERIALS |
| --- | --- | --- | --- |
| RESPONSIBILITY | NAME | FOR THE MEETING | |
| Minutes | | | |
| Housekeeping Issues | | | |
| | | | |
| | | | |
| | | | |

MISC. NOTES: ____________________________________________________________

________________________________________________________________________

________________________________________________________________________

# MEETING AGENDA

| TOPIC/GROUP | WHEN & WHERE |
|---|---|
| | DATE:     TIME:     PLACE: |

PHONE NUMBERS FOR QUESTIONS:     FOR THE CHAIRPERSON:

| ITEMS FOR DISCUSSION | ACTION EXPECTED | TIME IN MINUTES | LEAD/PH. EXT. |
|---|---|---|---|
| | | | |

## IMPORTANT INFORMATION

| PREPARATION NEEDED | PLEASE BRING |
|---|---|
| | |

© NOVA I, Ltd., 1991

# MEETING MINUTES

| TOPIC/GROUP: | CHAIRPERSON: |
|---|---|
| DATE:          TIME: | ATTENDANCE: ☐ See attached   ☐ As follows |
| PLACE: | |

| ISSUES DISCUSSED (LIST) | DECISIONS MADE |
|---|---|
| | |

| SPECIAL NOTES, COMMENTS, DISCUSSION | TO DO | WHO | WHEN |
|---|---|---|---|
| | | | |

**NEXT MEETING**   DATE:          TIME:          PLACE:

# FUTURE AGENDA RECORD

TOPIC / ISSUE: _______________________________

COMMENTS / NOTES: _______________________________

| AGENDA | ACTION NEEDED: | RESOURCES: (List) |
|---|---|---|
| DATE: | ☐ INFORMATION | |
| LEAD: | ☐ DISCUSSION | |
| TIME ALLOCATION: | ☐ DECISION | |
| | ☐ OTHER | |

---

TOPIC / ISSUE: _______________________________

COMMENTS / NOTES: _______________________________

| AGENDA | ACTION NEEDED: | RESOURCES: (List) |
|---|---|---|
| DATE: | ☐ INFORMATION | |
| LEAD: | ☐ DISCUSSION | |
| TIME ALLOCATION: | ☐ DECISION | |
| | ☐ OTHER | |

---

TOPIC / ISSUE: _______________________________

COMMENTS / NOTES: _______________________________

| AGENDA | ACTION NEEDED: | RESOURCES: (List) |
|---|---|---|
| DATE: | ☐ INFORMATION | |
| LEAD: | ☐ DISCUSSION | |
| TIME ALLOCATION: | ☐ DECISION | |
| | ☐ OTHER | |

# CHAIRPERSON SELF EVALUATION

TOPIC: _______________________________________________

DATES: From ______________ to ______________    # Meetings _______________

**MEETING TYPE:**
- ❑ TASK FORCE, AD HOC COMMITTEE/GROUP
- ❑ STANDING COMMITTEE, CONTINUING CAUSE
- ❑ BUSINESS MEETING
- ❑ OTHER: _______________________________

**MEETING LENGTH:**
- ❑ 1-2 HOURS
- ❑ 2-4 HOURS
- ❑ 4-8 HOURS

OTHER IMPORTANT NOTES: _______________________________________________

_______________________________________________

## DID YOU —

| | | | |
|---|---|---|---|
| 1. | Understand the reason for this meeting? | Yes ❑ | No ❑ |
| 2. | Believe this meeting was necessary? | Yes ❑ | No ❑ |
| 3. | Explain the purpose to the members? | Yes ❑ | No ❑ |
| 4. | Define expectations and rules of order? | Yes ❑ | No ❑ |
| 5. | Explain how the meetings were to be managed? | Yes ❑ | No ❑ |
| 6. | Define between-meeting communication? | Yes ❑ | No ❑ |
| 7. | Prepare for each meeting? | Yes ❑ | No ❑ |
| 8. | Arrive early to greet members and set the tone? | Yes ❑ | No ❑ |
| 9. | Assign specific responsibilities for preparation to the members? | Yes ❑ | No ❑ |
| 10. | Distribute agendas in advance? | Yes ❑ | No ❑ |
| 11. | Plan agenda time carefully? | Yes ❑ | No ❑ |
| 12. | Clearly communicate preparation expectations to all members? | Yes ❑ | No ❑ |
| 13. | Give all members a chance to contribute? | Yes ❑ | No ❑ |
| 14. | Rescue discussions from tangents? | Yes ❑ | No ❑ |
| 15. | Make sure the room was inviting and appropriately arranged for interaction? | Yes ❑ | No ❑ |
| 16. | Consider the needs of the group when scheduling the meeting? | Yes ❑ | No ❑ |
| 17. | Focus on what might work and what to try next? | Yes ❑ | No ❑ |
| 18. | Teach members how to meet expectations and complete actions needed? | Yes ❑ | No ❑ |
| 19. | Remind others of their responsibilities? | Yes ❑ | No ❑ |
| 20. | Believe in the group and what it could accomplish? | | |

| THINGS TO CHANGE | PEOPLE WHO CAN HELP |
|---|---|
| | |

# MEMBER SELF EVALUATION

## DID YOU —

1. Budget time for attendance *and* preparation when the meeting was scheduled? Yes ❑   No ❑

2. Let others know what you do well? Did you offer to help?   Yes ❑   No ❑

3. Review the agenda before each meeting?   Yes ❑   No ❑

4. Organize for contribution?   Yes ❑   No ❑

5. Help others prepare for the meeting?   Yes ❑   No ❑

6. Attend every meeting?   Yes ❑   No ❑

7. Were you on time for meetings?   Yes ❑   No ❑

8. Make sure your viewpoint was adequately understood?   Yes ❑   No ❑

9. Encourage examination of the other side?   Yes ❑   No ❑

10. Discourage generalizations?   Yes ❑   No ❑

11. Absorb the viewpoint of others?   Yes ❑   No ❑

12. Commit to the group?   Yes ❑   No ❑

13. Help others believe in the cause and the group enough to get involved?   Yes ❑   No ❑

14. Follow through on your commitments?   Yes ❑   No ❑

15. Redirect tangential discussions when they occurred?   Yes ❑   No ❑

16. Support established group rules?   Yes ❑   No ❑

| THINGS TO CHANGE | PEOPLE WHO CAN HELP |
| --- | --- |
|  |  |

# HOW DOES YOUR MEETING MEASURE UP?

## DIRECTION   A reason for meeting that's clear; leadership that shows.

_________ 1. Goals are simply and directly stated.
_________ 2. The members understand the primary purpose of the meeting.
_________ 3. The purpose is of high priority to the group and to the individuals involved.
_________ 4. The appointed chairperson is confident and able to aim the group and keep it on target and on time.
_________ 5. Participants are told what to expect and what's expected of them.

☐ TOTAL THIS SECTION

## PREPARATION   Plans to make the best use of time; performance that delivers.

_________ 6. Adequate time is allowed for preparation.
_________ 7. Agendas are distributed in advance; discussion items are identified so that preparation can occur.
_________ 8. Attempts are made to plan agenda time.
_________ 9. Meetings start and end on time.
_________ 10. Members prepare for the meeting and it shows.

☐ TOTAL THIS SECTION

## PARTICIPATION   Exchange that produces ideas; dialogue that promotes understanding.

_________ 11. It's easy to say what one feels; all members feel secure in expressing their opinions.
_________ 12. A willingness to examine all sides of the issue is present.
_________ 13. Everything is "equal" inside the meeting room; all sides of the issue are fairly represented.
_________ 14. Circadian cycles and conflicting events are considered when planning the meeting time.
_________ 15. Lighting, temperature control and seating arrangements are considered in advance; the "welcome mat" is out.
_________ 16. Members are usually on time for the meeting; people rarely leave early.
_________ 17. The meeting room is organized; attempts are made to arrange for participant eye contact.
_________ 18. Discussions are productive; the group gets to the "heart of the matter" quickly.
_________ 19. Interruptions are minimized; except for emergencies, pagers and phone calls are eliminated.

☐ TOTAL THIS SECTION

## ACTION   Commitment to achieve success; the power and expertise to make it happen.

_________ 20. Issues are important to the individuals involved.
_________ 21. Power to act exists; decisions that are made can be implemented.
_________ 22. Expertise needed for action, including first hand knowledge/experience with the issues central to the meeting, are present.
_________ 23. Action needed is clearly stated and consistently communicated.
_________ 24. Everybody _does_ what they say they're going to do.
_________ 25. Teamwork prevails. Problems are shared.

☐ TOTAL THIS SECTION

**SCORING KEY**
1 = Strongly disagree
2 = Disagree
3 = Agree
4 = Strongly agree

# THE BOTTOM LINE

## THE DATA

TOPIC:                                   DATES:   From          to

### ATTENDEES

| | | |
|---|---|---|
| (A) | NUMBER AT EACH MTG. | |
| (B) | AVERAGE HOURLY PAY | |
| (C) | PREP TIME PER MTG. | |

### MEETINGS

| | | |
|---|---|---|
| (D) | TOTAL # HELD | |
| (E) | AVG. LENGTH EACH MTG. | |
| (F) | TOTAL MTG. HRS. (D x E) | |

### SECRETARY

| | | |
|---|---|---|
| (G) | HOURLY PAY | |
| (H) | PREPTIME PER MTG. | |

## THE SCORE  *(From the Winning Hand)*

| | TOTAL |
|---|---|
| DIRECTION | |
| PREPARATION | |
| PARTICIPATION | |
| ACTION | |
| TOTAL | |

**85 – 100**
*Great job!*

**60 – 84**
*Time for attention*

↓ **60**
*Consider folding!*

## THE COST

### FOR ATTENDEES

| | |
|---|---|
| IN PREPARATION (A x B x C x D) | |
| IN MEETINGS (A x B x F) | |

### FOR SECRETARY

| | |
|---|---|
| PRE-MEETING (G x H x D) | |
| FOR THE MEETING (F x G) | |

### OTHER

| | |
|---|---|
| PAPER | |
| COPY SERVICE | |
| FOOD | |
| ROOM | |

## TOTAL COST: [        ]

## THE RESULTS

## LESSONS LEARNED